The Climb to Financial Freedom

A Motivational Guide

By: Kay Cunningham

"Watch your thoughts; they become words. Watch your words; they become actions. Watch your actions; they become habit." -Lao Tzu

*D*ebt & Poverty are correlated in my opinion and starts with a mindset which fosters behavior, then becomes a habit. To break this mindset and behavior, change is required. Change forces us to do something different, which yields a different result from what we have been getting.

Kay C.

Contents

Step 1

Debt, how did I get here?

Okay so the splurging on clothes, shoes, jewelry, latest fads and cars got you here now what?

Debt, often "finds most of us". It is at this stage in life that you must assess your current financial state and if overcome with debt, admit that you have trouble controlling your financial behavior.

On this day, you should gather all your documents to determine exactly how much is owed and exactly how much is needed to pay off your debt.

List Debt & Debt Amounts

1. _____

2. _____

3. _____

4. _____

5. _____

6. _____

7. _____

8. _____

Step 2

What is your Relationship With Money?

To get a proper understanding of your financial state, it is important to understand your money type. This will enable you to make better money choices.

Which Money type are you?

- **Are you an Image spender**, one who uses money in highly visible ways? Do you often pick up the tab, drive a flashy or prestigious vehicle and wear designer clothing?
- **Are you a Bargain-hunter**, someone who is all about "getting the deal"?
- **Are you a Compulsive shopper**, who uses shopping as a distraction from emotional feelings or instability?

- **Are you a Co-dependent spender,** someone who spends on others to win approval or their acceptance?
- **Are you a Bulimic spender**, a high earner who gets rid of their money (by spending) and return to a broke state because it feels comfortable?

Do you recognize yourself in any of these behaviors? I know I did.

The are many ways to make a conscious change regarding your money type. But the first and most important step is becoming aware of your actions and your current financial state. Once aware, a change in your behavior must follow. Behavior has three components: thoughts, feelings and actions. In order to change your behavior, you have to change all three, and they have to be consistent.

What's Your Money Type?

Step 3

Create A Life Resume

Just as you prepare a resume to yield a position of your liking, create a resume for your life. In your life resume; instead of listing your skill set, list your life expectations and what is required of you to achieve your desires. Define your purpose!

It is only with clarity that you can move on to the next step.

Life Resume

Objectives/Goals:

_____

_____

_____

Steps To Achieve Your Goals:

_____

_____

_____

Accomplishments:

_____

_____

_____

Step 4

Take The Fear Out of Finances

The phrase "Knowledge is Power and those who lack it will perish" is true to its saying, especially when it comes to debt. What you don't know may "cost" you in the long run.

When an offer involving money seems too good to be true in most instances, it is. There is no such thing as "Free Money".

Dedicate this day to learning and understanding new Money Terminology and revisiting those loan and credit card documents that were so quickly glanced over upon signing.

Do you understand how interest is calculated? Do you know the meaning of cash flow, expenses, assets, liabilities and net income?

Step 5

Prioritize Your Debt

Your Money Type has been noted, Life Resume written and Fear of Finances out the window. Next, rank your debts in order of size as this gives you a better perspective on how you can tackle your debt re-payment.

There are 2 options that you can choose from while on the climb to financial freedom. The first is the "snowball method", this is where the smallest debt is repaid first and the momentum from paying off the first debt propels you to eliminate the remaining debt.

The alternative method is by paying off the debt with the highest interest rate which ultimately allows you to pay less over the life of the loan.

It is important to make minimum payments on all your debts and extra when plausible.

Making a decision to tackle your debt can be an intimidating one, reach out to a financial advisor whenever you are unsure or confused on how to start this process.

List Debt by Priority

1. _____

2. _____

3. _____

4. _____

5. _____

6. _____

7. _____

8. _____

Step 6

Create a Realistic Budget

Now that you are mentally aware of your financial state, it's time to create a realistic Budget.

A Budget allows you to track how much money you have coming in and going out. This is an effective way of knowing exactly **WHAT** you are spending and **HOW** it is spent.

Budget Steps:

1. Identify your income and expenses.
2. Separate Needs & Wants
3. Design Your Budget
   (Unsure where to start? Try an easy to follow Online Template or a user-friendly budget template in Microsoft Excel)

List Your Needs & Your Wants

Needs	Wants

Step 7

Put Your Plan Into Action

Now that your budget is prepared, today is the day that you put your plan into action. Following a budget requires commitment, dedication and strong will. As each day passes, you should accurately record your expenses ensuring money is allocated for your necessities (housing, food, utilities, transportation, etc.) or you can choose to keep receipts until the end of the month and enter them in your spreadsheet at that time.

Getting on track with a budget can sometimes take a month or two. So, it is important to give yourself time to adjust.

What's Your Plan?

_____

_____

_____

_____

_____

_____

_____

_____

Step 8

Time of Sacrifice

The days to come will be some of the most challenging days that you will ever experience, but the result will be worth it. I promise you!

At this stage, every decision regarding making a purchase requires great scrutiny and will also call for sacrifice of Self. To gain in this process, you must give. You must give on the morning coffee from the big-name coffee houses, that takes an estimated $700.00 a year from you. You must give on the hearty lunch from the fast-food restaurants, that costs you an estimated $1,750.00 a year. You must give on the social activities and outings. You may also have to give on a little family time and take on a second job to help lower your debt.

What Will You Sacrifice?

1. _____

2. _____

3. _____

4. _____

5. _____

6. _____

7. _____

Step 9

The Dreaded "S" Word

At this point I know you are saying how can I Save when I'm barely trying to Survive?

However, as dreaded as the word savings is, it is so necessary for survival and living debt free. Most people find themselves in a financial rut because they do not have the funds needed in times of emergency and resort to credit cards or unsecured loans.

Have you ever heard of the saying a little goes a long way? Use this adage, when it comes to developing your savings. While it would be ideal to have 3 months' income saved, not everyone may be in a position to do so. I certainly wasn't!

You must condition your mind to the process of saving a little at a time, if only by saving your spare/loose coins. Remember, your thoughts become actions and your actions become habit.

Think about this:
Using the penny saving schedule:

Penny X # of day X 365 = $667.95
or
$5.00 X 365 Days = $1,825.00

For some, the payout may not be that great. But for others including myself, it was a lot more than what I started out with.

The point is to get started at a pace fitting to your circumstances. You have to be committed to saving, to build the funds needed to strengthen your financial security.

What are Your Savings Goals?

Goal 1:

$_____

Goal 2:

$_____

Goal 3:

$_____

Step 10
Become A Minimalist

Another part of sacrificing is minimalizing the need for unnecessary material possession.

LESS is MORE

Minimalism is the art of bringing to fruition the things we most value and the removal of everything that distracts us from it. Owning less, costs less and requires less use of your valuable time. It is this state that forces you to focus on what's important in life and make necessary improvements in areas that may require it.

Live A Life That Is Free!

Step 11

Live Within Your Means

Again, spending more than you earn is what causes you to become consumed with debt. You must be comfortable in your own lane, at your own pace. There is no need to compete with any one. Don't get caught up "keeping up with the Joneses".

I am sure your friends or neighbors might drive nicer cars, have the newest technology, or take expensive vacations, but that doesn't mean you must do the same. You don't know how they got to where they are or what their finances look like, people are master pretenders. Financing a vacation, taking out a loan for a new car and having multiple credit cards are major pitfalls that people make and you should avoid at all costs.

Live The Life That You Can Afford!

Step 12

Seek A New Opportunity

Every individual has been born with a gift. It is this gift that should provide for you, once tapped into.

Are you a great cook, baker, hairstylist, artist or cleaner? Whatever the talent, make it work for you. Use your talent to generate supplemental income.

Feeling a bit uneasy and not sure where to start? There are so many free resources available to you on the world-wide web. It all starts with a thought, a plan and action.

Invest In Yourself!

Step 13

Have A Sense Of Urgency

Are you someone who has no urgency to get things done, to achieve your goals, to overcome your problems?

There are many reasons that may have gotten you to this point, but your level of comfort is preventing you from moving forward in life.

A sense of urgency is required to help you to set S.M.A.R.T goals (Specific, Measurable, Achievable, Realistic, Time based) and work efficiently throughout your day. You must be consistent and persevere, if you wish to maintain the highest levels of performance in all aspects of your life. Get up, get out there and pursue your goals.

Step 14

Evaluate Your Circle

I am certain that you have heard the term "Eagles doesn't fly with pigeons". Simply put, this means that on the road to financial freedom it's imperative that you surround yourself with like-minded individuals.

Though you may not see it, the power of influence on your life by others should not be underestimated. Have you ever thought of an out of the box idea or decided to create something that hasn't been done before and you share this idea with your peers and get a not so favorable response? This is because your peers are evaluating you based upon their self-limiting beliefs.

Don't let their thoughts, deter you from your goal. What you should do instead, is share your goals and dreams with an inner circle of people who will deliver positive and constructive feedback, which will provide the motivation needed to launch your plans.

Step 15

Limit your Social Media Exposure

Unless advertising or promoting your business online, the amount of time spent on social sites should be minimal. I believe that too much time spent on social media correlates negatively with your wellbeing and happiness.

The world of social media has allowed individuals to connect to a distorted version of reality, which can distract you from pursuing your goals. Social Media does not show the struggles and lows in the lives of others but only promotes the highs and excitement.

It is important to know your worth, value yourself, accept your circumstances and make the necessary changes to your life as YOU see fit.

Final Step

Be Proactive, Not Reactive

Okay; your mind has been set, budget prepared, sacrifices made then life gets in the way and debt re-payment is not as easy as it seems. Now what?

The thing about life is, it does not matter how much we plan or try to go by the book; circumstances happen that are beyond our control.

While an unexpected expense or event may occur, and throw you off track, it is important to not get discouraged. Call your creditor and explain your circumstances to them; this action may allow room for a new repayment option. Financial avoidance and neglect is never okay, as it only compounds your issues.

Overcoming debt is a process that takes time. Fixate your mind on the overall goal and create the steps needed to get you to where you want to be.

There is no one size fit all solution to overcoming debt. This process requires you to be honest, committed and determined to press on no matter how it looks.

Are You Ready To Make The Climb?

www.ingramcontent.com/pod-product-compliance
Lightning Source LLC
Chambersburg PA
CBHW070426190526
45169CB00003B/1423